Contents

Some words are shown in bold, **like this**.
You can find them in the glossary on page 23.

What kind of pet is this?

Pets are animals that live with us.

Some pets are big and furry.

Pets in my house

Hamsters

Jennifer Blizin Gillis

www.raintreepublishers.co.uk
Visit our website to find out more information about **Raintree** books.

To order:
 Phone 44 (0) 1865 888112
 Send a fax to 44 (0) 1865 314091
Visit the Raintree Bookshop at **www.raintreepublishers.co.uk** to browse our catalogue and order online.

First published in Great Britain by Raintree, Halley Court, Jordan Hill, Oxford OX2 8EJ, part of Harcourt Education.
Raintree is a registered trademark of Harcourt Education Ltd.

Editorial: Catherine Clarke and Daniel Cuttell.
Design: Michelle Lisseter
Picture Research: Heather Sabel and Maria Joannou
Production: Amanda Meaden

Originated by Dot Gradations Ltd
Printed and bound in China by South China Printing Company

ISBN 1 844 43574 1 (hardback)
09 08 07 06 05
10 9 8 7 6 5 4 3 2 1

ISBN 1 844 43580 6 (paperback)
10 09 08 07 06
10 9 8 7 6 5 4 3 2 1

British Library Cataloguing in Publication Data
Blizin Gillis, Jennifer
Hamsters. – (Pets in my house)
636.9'356
A full catalogue record for this book is available from the British Library.

Acknowledgements
The publishers would like to thank the following for permission to reproduce photographs:
Animals Animals pp.8 (Robert Maier), 10 (Robert Maier), 15 (Jorg and Petra Wegner), 23(e) (John Maier); Arndt (Premium Stock/Picture Quest) pp.7, 23(a);Corbis pp.6, 23(b); Getty Images (PhotoDisc) pp.21, 22, 23(c), 23(d); Harcourt Education Ltd pp.4 (Robert Lifson), 5, 11 (Trevor Clifford), 17, 23(f), 23(g); Papilio (Robert Picket) pp. 9, 16, 20; Photo Edit p.13 (David Young-Wolff); Rob van Nostrand p.18; Tudor Photography pp.12, 14, 19.

Cover photograph reproduced with permission of Corbis (Robert Picket).

The publishers would like to thank Michaela Miller for her assistance in the preparation of this book.

Every effort has been made to contact copyright holders of any material reproduced in this book. Any omissions will be rectified in subsequent printings if notice is given to the publishers.

The paper used to print this book comes from sustainable resources.

My pet is small and furry.

Can you guess what kind of pet this is?

What are hamsters?

squirrel

Hamsters are **rodents**.

This means hamsters are in the same family as squirrels and mice.

In the wild, hamsters live under ground in **burrows**.

All hamsters are **nocturnal**.

Where did my hamster come from?

This mother hamster has had a **litter** of **pups**.

There are five brothers and sisters.

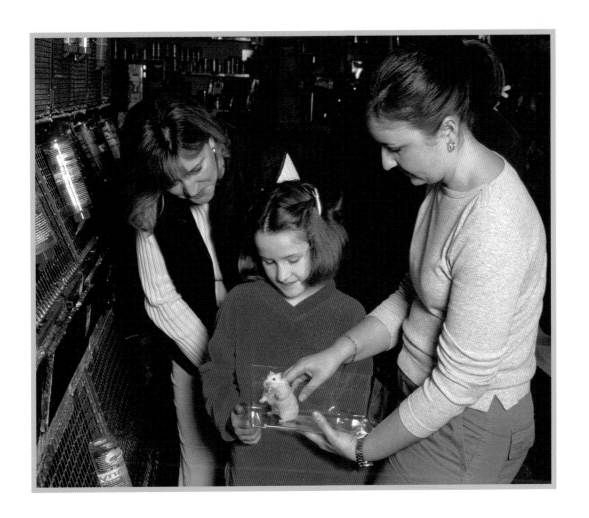

The pups stayed with their mother for four weeks.

Then, they went to new homes.

How big is my hamster?

When it was born, my hamster was very small.

It was about the size of my finger.

Now my hamster is grown up.

It is as big as my hands.

Where does my hamster live?

My hamster lives in a cage.

There is a wire lid to keep the hamster inside.

shavings

There are lots of **shavings** inside the cage.

The hamster uses these to make a **burrow**.

What does my hamster eat?

My hamster eats dry food.

I give it some food every day.

My hamster eats fruit and vegetables, too.

I give it very small pieces of apple, potato, carrot, and peas.

What else does my hamster need?

water bottle

A hamster needs lots of water.

I hang a water bottle in its cage.

A hamster needs a box to sleep in.

My hamster goes there to hide or to rest.

What can I do for my hamster?

I keep my hamster's home clean.

I change the **shavings** and clean out the cage at least once a week.

I can help my hamster get plenty of exercise.

I put a wheel inside its cage.

What can my hamster do?

My hamster can climb.

It has a special ladder in its cage.

My hamster has special **pouches** in its cheeks.

It saves food inside these pouches.

Hamster map

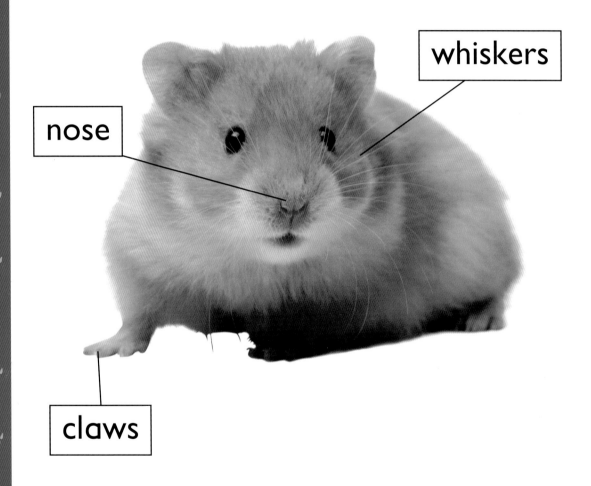

whiskers

nose

claws

Glossary

burrow
hole that an animal digs to make its home

litter
group of baby animals, such as dogs, cats, or hamsters

nocturnal
animal that is awake at night and sleeps in the day

pouch
part of an animal's body that can get bigger to hold food or babies

pup
baby hamster

rodent
small, furry animal with sharp teeth for chewing things

shavings
small pieces of paper or wood

Index